BANANAS IN MY EARS

A Collection of
Nonsense Stories,
Poems, Riddles, and Rhymes

First published in the U.K. as *Smelly Jelly Fish* (1986), *Under the Bed* (1986), *Hard-boiled Legs* (1987), and *Spollyollydiddlytiddlyitis* (1987), by Walker Books Ltd, 87 Vauxhall Walk, London SE11 5HJ

First U.S. edition 2012

Library of Congress Cataloging-in-Publication Data is available.

Library of Congress Catalog Card Number 2012938742

ISBN 978-0-7636-6248-6

13 14 15 16 17 GCP 10 9 8 7 6 5 4 3 2

Printed in Dongguan, Guangdong, China

This book was typeset Bembo.
The illustrations were done in ink and watercolor.

Candlewick Press
99 Dover Street
Somerville, Massachusetts 02144

visit us at www.candlewick.com

BANANAS IN MY EARS

A Collection of Nonsense Stories, Poems, Riddles, and Rhymes

Michael Rosen

illustrated by

Quentin Blake

CANDLEWICK PRESS

Contents

Hard-boiled Legs
The Breakfast Book

Smelly Jelly Smelly Fish
The Seaside Book

Spollyollydiddlytiddlyitis
The Doctor Book

Under the Bed
The Bedtime Book

Hard-boiled Legs

The Breakfast Book

Breakfast Time

Someone's dropped a bottle of milk.
The trashman's dropped a trash can.

Someone's found a piece of potato in their shoe.
The baby's eating a sock.
When is it?
Breakfast time.

The cat's on the table eating someone's bacon.

Someone's wiped butter on their pants.

Someone's poured tea into the sugar bowl.

The baby is eating eggshells.

When is it?

Breakfast time.

Someone thinks he's going to get very angry.

Someone thinks she's going crazy.

Someone thinks he's going to scream.

The baby has tipped cornflakes over her head.

When is it?

Breakfast time.

What If . . .

What if
a piece of toast turned into a piece of ghost
just as you were eating it
and you thought you were going to sink your
teeth into a lovely crunchy piece of hot toast
and butter and instead this cold wet feeling
jumps into your mouth
going,
"Whooooooooooooooooooooo!"
right down into your stomach

and your mom says,
"What did you say?"
You say, "Nothing, Mom,"
but the ghost sitting in your stomach
does it again.
"Whoooooooooooooooooooo!"
and everyone looks at you.

A Little Boy Came Down to Breakfast

A little boy came down to breakfast
with bananas stuck in his ears.

Everyone said hello to him
but he didn't take any notice.
So his mom said, "Are you all right?"
But the little boy said nothing.
So his sister said, "Are you all right?"
But the little boy still said nothing.

Then his brother noticed that he had bananas stuck in his ears, so he said, "Hey, you've got bananas stuck in your ears." And the little boy said, "What?" So his brother said it again. "You've got bananas stuck in your ears." And the little boy said, "What?" So the brother shouted really loudly at him, "YOU'VE GOT BANANAS STUCK IN YOUR EARS!" And the little boy shouted back, "I'M SORRY, I CAN'T HEAR YOU. I'VE GOT BANANAS IN MY EARS!"

Nat and Anna

Nat and Anna were having breakfast.

Mom said to Anna, "I'm just going upstairs
to get ready. Make sure Nat finishes his
breakfast, will you?"

Mom went out.

Nat got off his chair.

Anna said, "Sit down, Nat."

Nat said, "I'm going for a walk."

Anna said, "Sit down, Nat."

Nat came back and sat down.

Nat said, "I sat down, Anna. Can I get up now?"

Anna said, "Sit down, Nat."

Nat said, "I'm going to the beach."

Anna said, "Sit down, Nat."

Nat went under the table and sat down.

Nat said, "I'm sitting down now, Anna."

Anna said, "You can't sit there, Nat."

Nat said, "I'm having a picnic at the beach."

Anna said, "But you don't have a picnic with you."

Nat came out from under the table and sat down
on his chair.

Mom shouted from upstairs,
"Are you all right?"

Anna said, "Yes."

Nat got off the chair with a bowl of cornflakes.

Anna said, "What are you doing?"

Nat said, "I'm going to the beach with a picnic."

Anna said, "Sit down, Nat."

Nat got under the table and sat down with a
bowl of cornflakes.

Nat said, "I'm sitting down having my picnic
at the beach."

Anna said, "I'm going to pull you out of there, Nat."

Nat said, "You can't. You're not on the beach."

Anna said, "I can. Look."

Anna pulled Nat very hard.

The cornflakes and milk spilled all over the floor.

Mom shouted from upstairs,
"Everything all right?"

Nat said, "No."

Anna said, "You're going to get into trouble
now, Nat."

Mom came in.

Mom said, "What is going on? What's all this mess all over the floor?"

Nat said, "We're having a picnic at the beach, aren't we, Anna?"

Mom said, "Listen here, Anna. Next time I leave you alone like that, don't get Nat playing your silly games, do you understand? Now go to your room and stay there."

Anna walked out.

Nat said, "Can I go with her?"

Mom said, "No."

Anna said, "No, no, no, no, no, no, no, no, no, no, no."

Nat said, "Why is Anna shouting?"

What Happens Next?

If he steps on the dog . . .
If the dog tries to run . . .
If the table moves . . .
If the parrot . . .
If the man up the ladder . . .
OH, NO! OH, NO! OH, NO!

What If . . .

What if

hard-boiled eggs turned into hard-boiled legs

just when your dad was eating his egg

and he says,

"Hey, what's this?"

and the hard-boiled leg starts to run all round

the table and your dad starts to chase it.

"I want my egg!"

But the leg stands up and says,

    "You can't catch me.

      I'm no egg.

      You can't catch me.

      I'm a hard-boiled leg,"

and it runs out the door and your dad runs out
the door after it,
still wearing his pajamas.

Smelly Jelly Smelly Fish

The Seaside Book

On the Beach

There's a man over there,
and he's sitting in the sand.
He buried himself at teatime.
Now he's looking for his hand.

There's a boy over there,
and he's sitting on the rocks,
eating apple crumble,
washing dirty socks.

There's a woman over there,
sitting in the sea.
I can see her
but she can't see me.

There's a girl over there
and she's sitting on a chair.
Standing just behind her
is a big grizzly bear.

23

Over My Toes

Over my toes
goes
the soft sea wash
see the sea wash
the soft sand slip
see the sea slip
the soft sand slide
see the sea slide
the soft sand slap
see the sea slap
the soft sand wash
over my toes.

What If . . .

What if
they made children-sized diggers
and you could take them down to the beach
to dig really big holes
and great big sand castles
that the waves couldn't knock down.

What if
they made children-sized submarines
you could get into and go off underwater
looking at people's feet
and you could find old wrecked ships
and glide about
finding treasure.

What if
they made children-sized helicopters
that you took with you to the beach
so that you could take off in one of them
whenever you wanted to
and fly around above the beach
or up the cliffs
looking into those high-up caves
and swoop down again
toward the sea and some secret beach.

What if
they made children-sized ice-cream cones . . .

Things We Say

Nat and Anna

Nat and Anna were walking along the beach.

Anna said, "You've got to look out for jellyfish, Nat."

Nat said, "I *am* looking out for jellyfish, Anna."

Anna said, "They're enormous."

Nat said, "I know they are."

Anna said, "And they're very yellow."

Nat said, "I know they are."

Anna said, "And they sting."

Nat said, "Oh."

Anna said, "They sting very hard and it really hurts."

Nat said, "Oh."

Nat started to walk very slowly and he was looking at the sand very hard.

Anna said, "Come on, Nat. Keep up."

Nat said, "I am, Anna."

Anna said, "What's the matter, Nat?"

Nat said, "Nothing."

Anna said, "Are you worried about something, Nat?"

Nat said, "No."

Anna said, "Come on then."

Nat said, "Look out! That's a jellyfish, Anna! It's going to sting me. I want to go back! That's a jellyfish, Anna!"

Anna said, "Where?"

Nat said, "There!"

Anna said, "It's a piece of seaweed, Nat."

Nat went on walking very slowly,

looking at the sand very hard.

Anna said, "Stop there, Nat. Don't move."

Nat said, "I know. I can see it. I can see the jellyfish.

It's a really big one. It's going to sting me.

I want to go back, Anna."

Anna said, "Oh, it's flown away."

Nat said, "What's flown away?"

Anna said, "That seagull."

Nat said, "But *I'm* looking at the jellyfish. It's going to sting me! I want to go back, Anna! That's a jellyfish, Anna!"

Anna said, "Where?"

Nat said, "There!"

Anna said, "That's a piece of wood, Nat."

Nat went on walking very slowly.

Nat said, "Hey, Anna?"

Anna said, "Yes."

Nat said, "What's that?"

Anna screamed,

"*Yaaaaaaaaaaaaaaaaaaaaaaaaaaaa!*"

Nat said, "What's the matter?"

Anna said, "That's a jellyfish. Don't touch it, Nat.
Don't go anywhere near it, Nat. It's a jellyfish."

Nat said, "Anna?"

Anna said, "Don't talk, Nat. Don't say anything."

Nat said, "Anna?"

Anna said, "Don't move, Nat. Don't move. It's going
to sting me. I want to go back. It's a jellyfish, Nat!"

Nat said, "Anna, it's an old balloon."

Anna looked at it for a long time.

Anna said, "So? So what if it is?"

Nat and Anna went very quiet.

Anna said, "Are you afraid of jellyfish, Nat?"

Nat said, "A bit."

Anna said, "Me too."

Nat said, "Smelly jellyfish."

Anna said, "Smelly jelly smelly fish."

Three Girls

There were three girls, and they were going for
a walk along the beach till they came to a cave.
One of the girls says, "I'm going in."
So she goes in.

When she gets in, she sees a pile of gold
sitting on the rocks, so she thinks, "Yippee,
gold, all for me!" And she steps forward to
pick it up and a great big voice booms out,
"I'm the ghost of Captain Cox.
All that gold stays on the rocks."

So the girl runs out of the cave.

The second girl goes in, and she sees the gold
and she thinks, "Yippee, gold, all for me!"
And she steps forward to pick it up and the
great big voice booms out,
"I'm the ghost of Captain Cox.
All that gold stays on the rocks."

So the girl runs out of the cave.

Then the third girl goes in, and she sees
the gold and she thinks, "Yippee, gold,
all for me!" And she steps forward to pick
it up and the great big voice goes,
"I'm the ghost of Captain Cox.
All that gold stays on the rocks."
And the girl says,
"I don't care. I'm the ghost of Davy Crocket,
and all that gold goes in my pocket!"
and she runs out of the cave with the gold.

Spollyollydiddlytiddlyitis

The Doctor Book

Down at the Doctor's

Down at the doctor's
where everybody goes
there's a fat white cat
with a dribbly bibbly nose,
with a dribble dribble here
and a bibble bibble there,
that's the way
she dribbles her nose.

Down at the doctor's,
where everybody goes,
there's a fat black dog
with messy missy toes.
With a mess, mess here,
and a miss, miss there,
that's the way
she messes her toes.

Down at the doctor's,
where everybody goes,
there's a fat red parrot
who everybody knows.
With a hi-de-hi here,
and a how-de-how there,
that's the parrot
that everybody knows.

What If . . .

What if I went to the doctor's
and I was ill and I went into her little room
where she's got the toys in the corner
and she's lying on the bed
because she's ill
so she says,
"Hello, I'm really ill.
What's wrong with me?"

So I pick up the stethoscope
and the thermometer
and all the other things on her desk,
and I'm supposed to know what to do with them . . .
and I do!

I do know.

I'm there with the stethoscope listening,

and I'm testing and feeling,

       and I'm saying, "Well, Doctor,

       I'll tell you what's wrong with you.

       You've got spollyollydiddlytiddlyitis."

And she says, "I do?"

And I say, "What you need is

a bottle of Rottybottytex."

And she says, "Thanks, thanks a lot.
Look, I've got some other sick people here."
And she opens up a closet,
and hundreds of ill people
walk out of the closet,

and I'm testing and measuring and listening
for hours and hours, and all the time
it was me who was ill.

Things We Say

Nat and Anna

Nat and Anna sat in the waiting room with Mom.

Anna said, "When I grow up, I'm going to be a doctor."

Nat said, "When I grow up, I'm going to be a doctor."

Anna said, "I don't want you to be a doctor."

Nat said, "You can't stop me. Look, I'm a doctor."

Anna said, "No, you're not. You're Nat."

Nat said, "I'm Doctor Nat, the doctor."

Anna said, "So? I'm Doctor Anna."

Nat said, "I'm the doctor around here. You can be
a taxi driver."

Anna said, "I don't want to be a taxi driver."

Nat said, "You can be ill. You've got a headache."

Anna said, "I'm not playing this anymore, Nat."

Nat said, "I am. I'm Doctor Nat. I'm Doctor Nat."

Anna said, "You're not. You're Doctor Sick
because you're sick all the time."

Nat said, "I'm not sick all the time."

Anna said, "Doctor Sick Sick Sick."

Nat said, "You're getting really ill, Anna,
and I'm going to make you better."

Nat sat on Anna.

Anna said, "I'm not ill, I'm not ill, I'm not ill."

Mom looked up.

Mom said, "You are ill, Anna. That's why we've come to see the doctor, okay?"

Nat said, "Anna is Doctor Sick."

Anna said, "Next time you're ill, Nat, I'm going to be Doctor Jump and I'm coming to jump on you."

Nat said, "Don't, Anna."

Anna said, "Yes, I will. Jump jump jump all over you."

Nat sat and thought about Anna jumping on him.

Nat said, "Hey, Anna. Look, let's both be ill, eh?"

Anna said, "No, let's both be Doctor Jump."

Feeling Ill

Lying in the middle of the bed
waiting for the clock to change
flicking my toes on the sheets
watching a plane cross the window
staring at the glare of the light
smelling the orange on the table
counting the flowers on the curtain
holding my head with my hand
hearing the steps on the stairs
lying in the middle of the bed
waiting for the clock to change.

This Woman Went to the Doctor's

This woman went to the doctor's and she said,
"Doctor, my family, we keep thinking we're all
sorts of different things."
"Like what?" said the doctor.
"Sometimes I feel like a cat."
"When did you start feeling like this?" said the doctor.
"When I was a kitten," she said.

"Oh, yes," said the doctor. "Anything else?"

"Well, my husband," she said, "he thinks he's a bell."

"Ah," said the doctor, "tell him to give me a ring. Anyone else?"

"Yes," said the woman, "my little boy. He thinks he's a chicken."

"Why didn't you tell me this before?" said the doctor.

"We needed the eggs," said the woman.

"Any other problems?" said the doctor.

"Yes, I keep forgetting things."

"What did you say?" said the doctor.

"I don't know," said the woman. "I've forgotten."

Under the Bed

The Bedtime Book

Fooling Around

"Do you know what?"
said Jumping John.
"I had a bellyache,
and now it's gone."

"Do you know what?"
said Kicking Kirsty.
"All this jumping
has made me thirsty."

"Do you know what?"
said Mad Mickey.
"I sat in some glue,
and I feel all sticky."

"Do you know what?"
said Fat Fred.
"You can't see me.
I'm under the bed."

After Dark

Outside after dark,
trains hum and traffic lights wink,
after dark, after dark.

In here after dark,
curtains shake and closets creak,
after dark, after dark.

Under the covers after dark,
I twiddle my toes and hug my pillow,
after dark, after dark.

Things You Say

What If . . .

What if

my bed grew wings and I could fly away in my bed?

I would fly to the top of a high block of apartments,

look out over all the streets,

and then come floating slowly down to the ground.

I would fly to a misty island near Japan
and watch fishing boats cross the sea.

If my bed grew wings I would fly to a thick forest
where there was an old broken-down castle
that no one knew about, hidden in the trees.
And wherever I went
and whatever I saw,
all the time I was in my bed.

Things They Say

Nat and Anna

Anna was in her room.
Nat was outside the door.
Anna didn't want Nat to come in.

Nat said, "Anna? Anna? Can I come in?"
Anna said, "I'm not in."

Nat went away.
Anna was still in her room.
Nat came back.

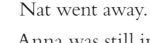

Nat said, "How did you say you're not in?
You must be in if you said you're not in."
Anna said, "I'm not in."
Nat said, "I'm coming in to see if you're in."
Anna said, "You won't find me because I'm not in."
Nat said, "I'm coming in."

Nat went in.

Nat said, "There you are. You are in."

Anna said, "Nat, where are you?
Where are you, Nat?"
Nat said, "I'm here."

Anna said, "I can't see you, Nat. Where are you?"
Nat said, "I'm here. Look."
Anna said, "Sorry, Nat. I can't see you."
Nat said, "Here I am. I'm going to scream, Anna.
Then you'll see me."
Anna said, "Where are you, Nat?"
Nat said, *"Yaaaaaaaaaaaaaaaaaaa!"*

Anna said, "I can hear you, Nat. But I can't see you."
Nat said, "Fine. I'm going out. Then you'll see me."

Nat went out.

Nat said, "Anna? Anna, can you see me now?"
Anna said, "No, of course I can't. You're outside."
Nat said, "Can I come in and see you then?"
Anna said, "But I'm not in."

Nat went away screaming.
He didn't come back.

These Two Children

There were these two children,
and they were in bed and it was
time they were asleep.

But they were making a huge noise,
shouting, yelling, and screaming.
"Look at me!" "Look at you!"
"Let's go mad!" "Yes, let's go mad!"

Their dad heard them and
he shouted up to them,
"Stop the noise! Stop the noise!
If you don't stop the noise, I'm
coming upstairs and I'll give
you some real trouble."

Everything went quiet.

A few minutes later one of the
children called out,
"Dad, Dad, when you come up to give
us some real trouble, can you bring
us up a drink of water as well?"

About the Author

Michael Rosen says, "What a clever fellow Quentin Blake is! I came to Walker Books one day and Quentin was sitting there with a scrappy piece of paper. On it was written a list of ideas: jokes, riddles, conversations, poems, things to do, cartoons . . . and that's how these poems came about. When I was a kid one of my favorite books was *The News Chronicle I-Spy Annual*. It would last me the whole year. I hope this book does the same for kids today."

Michael Rosen is one of the most popular authors of stories and poems for children. His titles include *We're Going on a Bear Hunt* (winner of the Smarties Book Prize), *Little Rabbit Foo Foo, Tiny Little Fly,* and *Dear Mother Goose.* He has written many collections of poetry including *Mind Your Own Business; Wouldn't You Like to Know; You Can't Catch Me!; Quick, Let's Get Out of Here;* and *Don't Put Mustard in the Custard,* all illustrated by Quentin Blake. He also compiled *Classic Poetry: An Illustrated Collection.* In 1997 he received the Eleanor Farjeon Award for services to children's literature and in 2007 he was appointed the British Children's Laureate.

Michael Rosen lives in London.

About the Illustrator

Quentin Blake says, "I have always liked Michael Rosen's poems; and what I particularly enjoy when I am illustrating them is that he seems to know everything about everyday life, but at the same time there is some fantasy that gets in as well."

Quentin Blake is a critically acclaimed children's book artist and was voted "The Illustrator's Illustrator" by *Observer* magazine. He is the illustrator of numerous Roald Dahl titles, several Michael Rosen poetry collections, *Michael Rosen's Sad Book,* and *The Rights of the Reader* by Daniel Pennac. He has also created many acclaimed picture books of his own, including *Mister Magnolia* (winner of the Kate Greenaway Medal), *All Join In* (winner of the Kurt Maschler Award) and *Clown* (winner of the Bologna Ragazzi Prize). In 1999 he was appointed the first British Children's Laureate.

Quentin Blake lives in London.

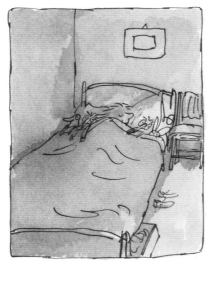